"But people themselves alter so much,
that there is something new
to be observed in them for ever."

"Follies and nonsense, whims and inconsistencies do divert me,
I own, and I laugh at them whenever I can."

"Think only of the past as its remembrance gives you pleasure."

> "It is a truth universally acknowledged, that a single man in possession of a good fortune, must be in want of a wife."

"There is a stubbornness about me that never can bear to be frightened at the will of others. My courage always rises at every attempt to intimidate me."

"I have been used to consider
poetry as the food of love."

"It is particularly incumbent on those who never change their opinion to be secure of judging properly first."

"Laugh as much as you choose, but you
will not laugh me out of my opinion."

"In vain have I struggled. It will not do.
My feelings will not be repressed.
You must allow me to tell you
how ardently I admire and love you."

"To be fond of dancing was a certain
step towards falling in love..."

"A lady's imagination is very rapid; it jumps from admiration to love, from love to matrimony, in a moment."

"The distance is nothing when one has a motive."

"I am the happiest creature in the world.
Perhaps other people have said so
before, but not one with such justice."

"Vanity and pride are different things, though the words are often used synonymously. A person may be proud without being vain. Pride relates more to our opinion of ourselves, vanity to what we would have others think of us."

UNION SQUARE & CO.
NEW YORK

UNION SQUARE & CO. and the distinctive Union Square Gift
logo are trademarks of Sterling Publishing Co., Inc.

Union Square & Co., LLC, is a subsidiary of Sterling Publishing Co., Inc.

© 2025 Union Square & Co., LLC

All rights reserved. No part of this publication may be reproduced,
stored in a retrieval system, or transmitted in any form or by any means
(including electronic, mechanical, photocopying, recording, or otherwise)
without prior written permission from the publisher.

ISBN 978-1-4549-5997-7

For information about custom editions, special sales, and premium
purchases, please contact specialsales@unionsquareandco.com.

Printed in India

2 4 6 8 10 9 7 5 3 1

unionsquareandco.com

Cover design by Igor Satanovsky and Kaylie Pendleton
Interior design by Christine Heun

Cover and interior images: Feodora_21/Shutterstock.com (flowers);
marbled endpaper background: Andy Magee/Shutterstock.com